by Victor Gentle and Janet Perry

Gareth Stevens Publishing
A WORLD ALMANAC EDUCATION GROUP COMPANY

Please visit our web site at: www.garethstevens.com
For a free color catalog describing Gareth Stevens Publishing's
list of high-quality books and multimedia programs,
call 1-800-542-2595 or fax your request to (414) 332-3567.

Library of Congress Cataloging-in-Publication Data

Gentle, Victor.
    Leopards / by Victor Gentle and Janet Perry.
        p. cm. — (Big cats: an imagination library series)
    Includes bibliographical references and index.
    Summary: An introduction to the physical characteristics and behavior of the leopard,
a smart predator that can climb trees and that lives in a variety of environments.
    ISBN 0-8368-3026-1 (lib. bdg.)
    1. Leopard—Juvenile literature. [1. Leopard.] I. Perry, Janet, 1960- II. Title.
QL737.C23G48   2002
599.75'54—dc21   2001049694

First published in 2002 by
Gareth Stevens Publishing
A World Almanac Education Group Company
330 West Olive Street, Suite 100
Milwaukee, WI 53212 USA

Text: Victor Gentle and Janet Perry
Page layout: Victor Gentle, Janet Perry, and Tammy Gruenewald
Cover design: Tammy Gruenewald
Series editor: Catherine Gardner
Picture Researcher: Diane Laska-Swanke

Photo credits: Cover © Fritz Pölking/Visuals Unlimited; p. 5 © Mary Ann McDonald/McDonald
Wildlife Photography; p. 7 Keith Scholey/BBC Natural History Unit; p. 9 © Dr. Maurice G.
Hornocker/NGS Image Collection; p. 11 © E. A. Kuttapan/BBC Natural History Unit; p. 13
© Gerald & Buff Corsi/Visuals Unlimited; p. 15 © Lynn M. Stone/BBC Natural History Unit; p. 17
© Anup Shah/BBC Natural History Unit; p. 19 © Tom & Pat Leeson; p. 21 © Alan & Sandy Carey

Printed in the United States of America

1 2 3 4 5 6 7 8 9 06 05 04 03 02

Front cover: Most big cats do not climb
trees, but this leopard rests in a sunny spot
and gazes over the savanna.

TABLE OF CONTENTS

Words that appear in the glossary are printed in **boldface** type the first time they occur in the text.

SPOTS FOR LEOPARDS

Leopards can live in many different places. Their spotted fur suits them well in deserts, mountains, rain forests, or grasslands. Some leopards can even live near cities, close to human beings — their most dangerous enemies!

No matter where leopards call home, they learn the best way to make their living. They know how to fit into the neighborhood. Leopards can **adapt**.

Leopards **rasp** to call their **cubs**. Leopards do not roar or meow. They sound more like a lizard or a kid with a very sore throat.

SPOTS IN THE MIDDLE

Leopards are **predators**. They hunt other animals, their **prey**, for food. Like all cats, adult leopards eat only meat. Often, leopards share hunting grounds with other predators, such as lions and wild dogs. Other predators can make problems for a leopard.

But leopards are smart. They try to keep clear of these problem neighbors. Leopards hunt different prey and at different times of the night or day than their neighbors do. They also climb trees to hide, or **cache**, their food where other predators cannot reach it.

Using its strong shoulders, a leopard drags a **Tommy** into a tree. The leopard is almost the same size as the Tommy — about the same weight as a big deer.

MOUNTAIN DESERT SPOTS

To catch prey, leopards need to blend in. Their colors and patterns match the places they live in. Leopards that live on dry, rocky, treeless mountains have pale yellow fur scattered with spots.

Mountain leopards hunt mice, rabbits, sheep, and goats. Mice and rabbits scurry into holes. Sheep and goats leap up steep walls.

The leopard's hard-to-see coat helps it sneak up on its prey. Then, with a powerful leap and a chomp of its jaws, the leopard has a meal.

A Siberian leopard matches the colors and shadows of mountain dust and rocks. When leopards lie low and still, they are hard to see.

JUNGLE SPOTS

Jungles are hot, wet places that get lots of rain all year. Plants grow so thickly and animals grow in such great numbers that they cannot be counted. Jungles are filled with yummy prey for leopards.

Tigers live in jungles, too. They hunt large prey. Jungle leopards do not like to tangle with tigers. Instead, leopards choose small prey — insects, wild pigs, and small deer. Tigers are not great tree climbers. Leopards are! Safe from tigers on the ground, leopards can easily hunt monkeys in the trees.

A jungle leopard holds its dinner — a small deer. Its coat is orange, and it is surrounded by green leaves, but its spots hide it well in the shadows.

SAVANNA SPOTS

African leopards live in large, grassy areas, called **savannas**. Savanna leopards share hunting grounds with lions, African wild dogs, jackals, **hyenas**, and cheetahs. All of these animals, except cheetahs, steal food from each other. Lions and wild dogs also hunt leopards.

To stay away from these dangers, leopards hunt at different times and places than other predators hunt. Wild dogs hunt warthogs and Tommies during the day. Leopards hunt warthogs and Tommies, too, but they hunt in the middle of the night. At dusk and dawn, lions hunt zebras and **wildebeests**.

A leopard **stalks** through grass. Mother leopards may hunt during the day. Daytime is also the best time to hunt in rainy seasons.

CITY SPOTS

City dwellers in places like Beijing, China, and Bangkok, Thailand, have interesting neighbors. Leopards prowl the city edges for mice and birds. But there are very few records of leopards killing people.

In fact, leopards are careful to hide from human neighbors. A leopard can hunt near a city for a long time before people notice. When people find dead birds and mice, they blame house cats. They are shocked to find that the hunter is a leopard!

See the spots on this black leopard? A black leopard hunting at night would be hard to spot — even near a city!

CATS SPOTTED, DOING THIS AND THAT

Some leopards have learned special tricks to catch prey. Indonesian island leopards living on Bali know how to catch fish — and that is all they eat.

Other leopards know a trick that scares monkeys right out of their trees. During the night, a leopard bothers the monkeys by pulling at tree branches for hours. The frightened monkeys screech and leap about, getting no sleep. Finally, a tired monkey misses a branch and falls to the leopard's hungry jaws.

These cubs have found food, but will they be able to pull the tortoise out of its shell? Leopards do find ways to eat even the toughest prey.

MAKING MORE SPOTS

Like almost all cats, leopards hunt and sleep alone. A leopard **marks** its home area, or **territory**, with its scent. Marking tells other leopards that an area is taken.

Marking also tells males that females are ready to have cubs. Males and females get together to **mate** for a few days, then they go their own ways.

In three months, one to four cubs are born. The cubs stay with their mother for about a year. Then, young males leave and hunt on their own. The grown females may hunt inside their mother's territory, but not alongside their mother.

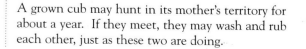

18

A grown cub may hunt in its mother's territory for about a year. If they meet, they may wash and rub each other, just as these two are doing.

LET THE WILD SPOTS BE!

Leopards kill other animals, but they do not waste what they kill. They fit into territories with other predators. Leopards do not threaten us.

Some people kill leopards for fur. People do not need leopard fur, and they waste a beautiful animal to get it. Other people take over the land where leopards hunt. Leopards have learned to adapt to many challenges. But leopards will not be able to survive if we do not change our ways.

Black leopards are born in the same litters as light ones. Both shades hide cubs well from predators — even humans!

MORE TO READ, VIEW, AND LISTEN TO

Books (Nonfiction)   *Big Cats* (series). Victor Gentle and Janet Perry (Gareth Stevens)
How to Hide a Polar Bear & Other Mammals. Ruth Heller
   (Grosset & Dunlap)
The Lookalikes. Anne Orth Epple (St. Martin's Press)
Mammals: The Hunters. Christopher O'Toole and John Stidworthy
   (Facts on File)
Save the Snow Leopard. Jill Bailey (Steck-Vaughn)

Books (Activity)   *Egg-Carton Zoo*. Rudi Haas and Hans Blohm (OUP)

Books (Fiction)   *The Bollo Caper*. Art Buchwald (Putnam)
Counting Leopard's Spots and Other Animal Stories. Hiawyn Oram
   (Little Tiger)

Videos (Nonfiction)   *Beauty and the Beasts: A Leopard's Story*. (National Geographic)
Predators of the Wild: Cheetah and Leopard. (Warner Home Video)

Audio (Fiction)   *How the Leopard Got His Spots*. (Rabbit Ears Storybook Classics)

PLACES TO VISIT, WRITE, OR CALL

Leopards live at the following zoos. Call or write to the zoos to find out about their leopards and their plans to preserve leopards in the wild. Better yet, go see the leopards, person to cat!

Lincoln Park Zoo
2200 North Cannon Drive
Chicago, IL 60614
(312) 742-2000

Sedgewick County Zoo
5555 Zoo Boulevard
Wichita, KS 67212-1698
(316) 942-2213

Memphis Zoo
2000 Prentiss Place
Memphis, TN 38112
(901) 276-WILD

Santa Barbara Zoological Gardens
500 Ninos Drive
Santa Barbara, CA 93103
(805) 963-5695

WEB SITES

Web sites change frequently, but we believe the following web sites are going to last. You also can use a good search engine, such as **Yahooligans!** [*www.yahooligans.com*] or **Google** [*www.google.com*], to find more information about leopards, other big cats around the world, and their homes. Some keywords that will help you are: *leopards, savannas, cats, African wildlife, zoo animals,* and *endangered species.*

www.yahooligans.com
Yahooligans! is a great research tool. It has a lot of information and plenty to do. Under Science and Nature, click on Animals and then click on The Big Picture: Animals. From there, you can try Animal Videos, Endangered Animals, Animal Bytes, BBC Animals, or Natural History Notebooks and search for information on leopards, savannas, jungles, mountains, and African or Asian wildlife.

www.pbs.org/kratts/
Visit *Kratt's World.* Go to the Creature World map and click on a continent to see what other animals live side by side with leopards.

library.thinkquest.org/12353
Thinkquest will show you what other kids are finding out and writing about leopards. Just click on African Mammals.

www.super-kids.com
Super-Kids will take you to games and pictures of big cats, along with other information about big cats. Start by clicking on Animals. Then try Africa, Monkeys, Tigers, or Zoos.

www.leopardsetc.com/meet.html
Leopards, Etc. lets you hear big cats. Click on the speaker icon next to each cat name. You can hear all kinds of big cats roaring, growling, rasping, barking, and purring.

www.nationalgeographic.com/features/ 97/cats/
National Geographic has a really cool game that lets you design the perfect predator.

www.nhm.org/cats/
The Natural History Museum of Los Angeles County has a really great exhibit called *Cats! Mild to Wild.* Click on Biology, and you will find how cats are built, how they use their claws, teeth, legs, and voices — and more!

www.kidsplanet.org
Kids' Planet by Defenders of Wildlife has many things to do. Click on Games for fun, or the Web of Life Story to learn how cats fit into our world, or Defend It to find out how to help stop people from killing leopards.

GLOSSARY

You can find these words on the pages listed. Reading a word in a sentence helps you understand it even better.

adapt (uh-DAPT) — to change, to make the best of changes in surroundings 4, 20

cache (KASH) — to hide or store food 6

cubs (KUHBZ) — big cats' babies 4, 16, 18, 20

hyenas (hye-EE-nuhs) — four-footed animals that look something like big dogs 12

marks (MARKS) — leaves a scent or scratches to warn other animals that a territory already belongs to a leopard 18

mate (MAYT) — to come together to make babies 18

predators (PRED-uh-turs) — animals that hunt other animals for food 6, 12, 20

prey (PRAY) — animals that are hunted by other animals for food 6, 8, 10, 12, 16

rasp (RASP) — to make a harsh, grating sound (see Web Sites, page 23) 4

savannas (suh-VAN-uhs) — large, grassy areas with few trees and little water 12

stalks (STAWKS) — to quietly follow prey 12

territory (TER-uh-tor-ee) — an area of land that an animal (or group of animals) marks out as its hunting ground 18, 20

Tommy (TAHM-ee) — a nickname for a Thomson's gazelle, which is a four-footed animal like a deer, with long, twisted horns and reddish brown fur on its back; plural: **Tommies** (TAHM-eez) 6, 12

wildebeests (WIHL-duh-beests) — four-footed animals with hooves, curly horns, and dark brown fur, like a small buffalo 12

INDEX

24